Other Books by Gabe Berman

Live Like a Fruit Fly:
The Secret You Already Know

Where Is God
When Our Loved Ones Get Sick?

The Complete Bullshit-Free
and Totally Tested Writing Guide:
How To Make Publishers, Agents, Editors
& Readers Fall In Love With Your Work

The Fifth Force

Love Looks Like This

Gabe Berman

Published by:
5-12 Media
East Rockaway, NY

ISBN: 978-0-692-66538-1

Cover and Interior Design:
The Book Couple • www.thebookcouple.com

Printed in the United States of America

*To everyone
who hasn't had a book
dedicated to them yet.*

Why are you here?

Wait.

I'm not asking, "Why are you holding this book right now?"

The answer to that is totally obvious. You're holding this book right now because, like me, you're madly in love.

Madly in love with love.

What I want to know is, why are you here? As in, why do you exist? What's your purpose?

I was on a quest to figure this out for most of my life.

It was my holy grail.

In the meantime, I resorted to what resonated with me: writing little poems, taking photos, and sharing both with friends and family.

These moments of losing myself in the spaces between words and shutter clicks surprisingly felt like being in love.

Yes, being in love.

And what's better than that?

Nothing.

Upon realizing this, my purpose was revealed.

I'm here to witness beauty. I'm here to add beauty.

That's it. That's why I exist.

And since you're holding this book right now, I'm pretty sure we're on similar paths.

You just read the introduction. I didn't label it as such because if you're anything like me, you would have skipped right past it.

Time stops, completely
when my calm, inner essence
sees itself in you.

I'm caused to love you.
How does resisting this feel?
I have no idea.

Love is the wormhole
through the universe which binds
us to the sacred.

The same current flows
equally through everything.
Feel it in stillness.

If enlightenment
were any closer to you,
you'd cease to exist.

I suddenly sensed
your intoxicating soul
in sunflower leaves.

A lotus flower
floats fredy on the surface
of my lover's dreams.

All of our lives
are lived one breath at a time,
no matter the plans.

There's a fearless force
woven into all atoms.
Soak yourself in it.

Who am I right now?
A dandelion spreading
its soul everywhere.

We are particles
of recycled, ancient stars
graced with awareness.

Regardless of age,
lovers abide timelessly,
in each other's arms.

Achieve mastery
in each moment you allow
silence to prevail.

Our minds became still
when a ladybug landed
in meditation.

Abide fearlessly
by sensing everything and
everyone as you.

Our steps are flawless
since the universe is the
choreographer.

I choose weightlessness
in response to the force of
your heart's gravity.

Let's welcome this breath.
Let's welcome every surprise.
All is intended.

I breathe in the chants
which were expelled from the lungs
of ancient prophets.

God's voice can be heard
in silent sunbeams creeping
across the dirt floor.

The pulse in your wrist
is synchronized with the hum
of all creation.

Each moment with you
feels like the last ten seconds
before the new year.

Dripping icicles.
Birds perched on leafless branches.
I sit and we breathe.

Both of these are true:
No two snowflakes are the same.
None are separate.

My father's footsteps
were once parallel to mine
on this quiet beach.

The water fountain
near the end of the boardwalk
tastes like summertime.

Throughout the winter,
seagulls from the beach glide
  through
my sleepy daydreams.

Fully formed haikus
reveal themselves gracefully
to silent poets.

If I could write the
loveliest of all haikus,
I'd write it for you.

My love is now yours.
It's as soothing as sun rays,
endless as the sky.

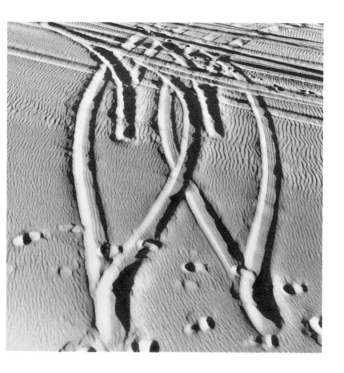

- You see me as a man, sitting
in a chair, drinking a cup of
coffee. But behind that, I am
a leaf, in a lake, surrendered
to its subtle current.

- I love you no matter what.
Love you no matter what.
Love you no matter.
Love no matter.
Love.

- If I were to write a love story, it would only be twelve words long: They were sucker punched by their love for each other. The end.

- I was making preparations
to love you long before we met.
Long before the universe took
shape. And long before even that.

- The twinkle in my eye recognizes the twinkle in yours. We've known each other before we knew ourselves.

- Poets and sages may never
speak of this moment again, but
rest assured, God's fingerprints
were left behind everywhere.

- Neither of us know the steps,
but something so insignificant
shouldn't keep us from dancing.

- While the sunlight illuminates
this moment, let's take a photo
of us looking at these old
photos of us and one day it
will be an old photo too.

- The sudden rainstorm ruined
a perfect summer day for some,
but the universe cooed over two
strangers sharing an umbrella.

- The monks have been silent
for many moons, but I hear
their chants in your heartbeat.

- Ones and zeros are convenient, but I only allow X's and O's to consume me.

- I'm writing these words in your past and you're reading them in my future. But yet, it's all happening right now.

How very lovely.

And since we're here, I'll use this moment, whenever it occurred or is occurring, to say that you're perfect.

As is.

There's nothing to strive to become.

Right now you are absolutely, undeniably perfect.

Let's take a deep breath together. Thank you.

- God smiles at you with
my lips.

- Evolution is dependent upon our smiles. Although I have no proof of this, I smile often just in case.

- I was once told, "Love isn't everything."

Those words sat with me for many months.

And now I know she was right. It's the only thing.

- Commit fully to a romance
with your heartbeat. Just sit in
awe of your own consciousness.

- Their hearts were like
active volcanoes. Exploding
violently, uncontrollably,
and unconditionally in all
directions. Leaving lakes
of molten love for all to
simmer in.

- My love for you hinges on
nothing. It's the same love
causing flowers to bloom.

- What's your purpose?

To love with the confidence
of a sunrise.

- You will decompose before
your work clothes.

- You're a collection of 100 trillion cells absorbed in many stories you've been told over your lifetime. But please remember, you're really just a collection of 100 trillion cells and the stories are just stories. Travel lightly.

- There's only love. All else
is theater.

- You see skin and hair and
lips and eyes, but please don't
let appearances deceive you.
I am nothing but heart.

- Enlightenment?

I have no thoughts which
bring me there.

Dear Reader,

I love you.

Yes, you.

The person reading these words right now.

I don't care if you're male or female, old or young, straight or gay, white or black, yin or yang, I love you.

Really, I do.

I am so in love with your essence, just thinking about it simultaneously wrecks and rebuilds me.

What do I mean by your essence?

It's that mysterious force which animates all of life. It flows with such gentleness. Such grace. And yet, such power.

And, in this moment, it's all I sense in you. Because it's being sensed with the exact awareness created by the same mysterious, all pervasive force.

But let's not get anchored with concepts.

Please just know, down to your bones and beyond, you are loved.

Right now, regardless of how you feel or what you've been told, you are loved.

Unconditionally. Unequivocally. Unrelentingly.

Underneath all of your feelings, emotions, thoughts, reactions, and judgments, you are loved like a mother loves her child. Like a poet loves his poems. Like sunbeams love flowers.

No questions, exceptions, or expectations.

Please allow yourself to allow me this.

Although, I will love you anyway.

Every way.

Thank you,
gb

Gabe is a writer, photographer, philosopher, and coffee drinker currently living on Long Island, New York.